THE SEVEN DWELLING PLACES OF GOD IN THE BIBLE

BY JAMES STEVENS

TATE PUBLISHING, LLC

The Seven Dwelling Places of God in the Bible
by James Stevens

Published in the United States of America
by Tate Publishing, LLC
127 East Trade Center Terrace
Mustang, OK 73064
(888) 361–9473

ISBN: 1-5988600-5-4

I lovingly dedicate this book to my wife Misty, who continually encouraged me to pursue the dream of writing my first book. Without your prayers, help, and support I could not have done it. I love you honey and want to say thank you!

TABLE OF CONTENTS

INTRODUCTION

O n Sunday night January 5, 2003, my life was changed. I had just come home from preaching a sermon on Revelation chapter 7. I could not stop thinking about what verse 15 said, *"Therefore they are before the throne of God, and serve Him day and night in His temple. And He who sits on the throne will dwell among them."* While I was preaching that night, the idea of Jesus dwelling with us in heaven impacted me in a powerful way. I had read the verse dozens of times before, but I had never grasped it in all of its fullness. Have you ever been reading a Bible verse or passage you had read many times before and all of a sudden it reached out and grabbed you? That is what happened to me. Later that night before going to bed, the Lord was still speaking to my heart about the verse. This led me to start thinking about other verses in the Bible that spoke of Him dwelling with His people. So I picked up my Bible and started in Genesis and went all the way through to Revelation looking for this idea. To my amazement, I saw it throughout the whole Bible. I had finally figured out for myself, all God has ever wanted is to be with His creation. And it got even better, upon further study I noticed that there are seven distinct places in the Bible where God has, is, and will dwell with His people. Overcome with a great sense of awe, I immediately started writing them down and here they are.

CHAPTER 1

The Garden of Eden

*"And they heard the sound of the LORD God
walking in the garden in
the cool of the day, and Adam and his wife hid
themselves from the presence
of the LORD God among the trees of the garden."*
GENESIS 3:8

It was the latter part of the day, and God was on His way down to visit with Adam and Eve. But this was unlike any other day, for on this particular day they weren't waiting for Him. Instead, they were hiding from His presence. We assume from scripture that up to this point, Adam and Eve had been experiencing fellowship with

God on a daily basis. When God visited them, it was always a special time. It was during these times that God revealed Himself in a personal and intimate way. What must it have been like to get visits from God? Why, it must have been a tremendous privilege for them to have God come and dwell in their midst.

God placed Adam and Eve in a peaceful and perfect place called the Garden of Eden (Genesis 2:8). While being in such a wonderful environment, they had the privilege of getting visits from Him. It is evident that God in His omniscience knew exactly where they lived and how to get there. Their location was more than just a small dot on earth's map to Him; it was probably highlighted with a star. I want to encourage you with this thought, with over five billion people on the earth today; God knows exactly where you are. And just as He stopped in to see Adam and Eve, He wants to do the same with you.

It is not only important that God knew where they lived, but also that He set aside the time to visit with them. We live in the twenty first century and people are busier now than ever. The society we live in today has become so fast paced that it has forgotten what is most important. God and our families! But thanks be to God, for He was never too busy that He couldn't take time out to visit with Adam and Eve. As their father, He knew how important it was to spend time fellowshipping with His children. In spite of His busy schedule of keeping all of creation in balance, He came to see them (Colossians 1:16). God has more responsibilities than we could ever imagine, but praise be to God that He controls all things. Just as He thought enough of Adam and Eve to come down and spend His precious time with them, He also wants to do the same with you and me today.

Not only did they have the privilege of

getting visits from God, but they also were able to experience His personal presence. God made it a priority to personally appear when visiting, *"and Adam and his wife hid themselves from the presence of the LORD,"* Genesis 3:8. God could have very well sent one of His angels to speak with them on His behalf. Angels throughout the Bible have always been God's ambassadors or representatives. For example, when Mary was given the glorious news that she would bear the Son of God, God did not come to deliver the news in person but sent His angel Gabriel. God did not utter the greatest words ever heard by human ears, *"He is not here, but is risen"* Luke 24:6. Instead, He sent an angel to proclaim this wonderful news. But instead of sending one of these heavenly ambassadors to visit Adam and Eve, He came Himself. All that He has ever wanted is to be with His people. That is the very reason why

He created you and me, so that He could personally spend each and every day with us.

When God did visit, He came near Adam and Eve. Genesis 3:8 states, *"And they heard the sound of the LORD God walking in the garden,"* meaning that God was very close by. I want you to think about someone who is going to see a famous person perform. Upon entering the arena, he finds his seat in the audience among thousands and sits down. When the concert begins, the famous person comes out and starts the show. It would be very unlikely that the star of the show would stop performing, walk down to where the spectator is, and start a conversation.

Famous people have always had a following of fans; perhaps all these fans wanted was an autograph, picture, or just the right to say they had met a celebrity. We live in a day and time that places great emphasis on movie stars, musicians, athletes, and everything Hollywood. Most everybody could name someone famous whom they would like to meet, and have the chance to be around. This is the same way God felt about Adam and Eve. They were famous in His eyes, and all He wanted was to be around them. And you know, He also feels the same way towards you and me. It is so awesome to think that even though we're not all famous, God wants to be with us more than we want to be with Him.

How wonderful it must have been for Adam and Eve to get personal visits from God, but what made it even better was the fellowship they were having with Him. God's coming to spend time with them, showed that He was truly interested in them. People like to feel important and needed. Showing an interest in someone is definitely one of the best ways to make them feel special. God's love for His creation is immeasurable; no finite person could ever comprehend such a love. As their father, He wanted them to know they were very important to Him. As a father myself, I realize how important it is for my children to understand how much I truly care about them. I have also realized spending time with my children is helping them build strong self-esteem and confidence. It must have been a very special experience for Adam and Eve to have a father who was involved in every aspect of their lives. Did you know that He also desires to be involved in every aspect of your life also? Are you letting him? If not, I encourage you to invite Him into your life today.

As a result of God showing an interest in the lives of Adam and Eve, this opened a door for communication. God talked with Adam while he was in the garden, *"And the LORD God commanded the man, saying,"* Genesis 2:16. He also wanted to hear what Adam had to say (Genesis 3:11). As humans we can be around people all the time, and never really talk with them. For example, a husband and wife that are married can live in the same house and talk with each other everyday but never truly communicate. This is the typical type of marriage today. It takes two people to have a conversation, one talks while the other listens, or vice versa. God desired to have an open line of communication with Adam and Eve. He wanted to talk with them as well listen to what they had to say. It is important for us to know that we can come to God and talk with Him about anything at anytime. My wife and I have always told our kids that they can come and talk with us about anything at anytime, and we promised to listen. As we have done this, we have been able to gather information that has helped us in keeping a healthy relationship. This is what God wanted with Adam and Eve and desires to have with you. Have you ever wondered what they talked with God about? Perhaps it was just a casual conversation on how their day was going, or about how they felt. Whatever they discussed was important to them, therefore it was also important to God. They could confide in Him their hopes and dreams, their desires and ambitions, but most of all their everyday ordinary life. Overall, they experienced what I would call a little of heaven on earth as a result of having God dwell in their midst.

Adam and Eve had everything that a person could ever want. They had the perfect life, place, body, and relationship with God. But as a result of their disobedience to God, they lost all of this and were kicked out of the garden of Eden (Genesis 3:22–24). God had commanded them in Genesis 2:17–18, *"Of every tree of the garden you may freely eat ; "but of the tree of the knowledge of good and evil you shall not eat."* Adam and Eve knew what they did was wrong, *"and Adam and his wife hid themselves from the presence of the Lord God among the trees of the garden"*

Genesis 3:8. I want to ask you right now: Are you hiding anything from God? Is there anything in your heart today that is keeping you from having true fellowship with Him? If so, would you pause right now and ask God for forgiveness? Amen. God wants so much to dwell with us, but we must be careful not to do as Adam and Eve, and hide from His presence.

CHAPTER 2

The Tabernacle of Meeting

*"And let them make Me a sanctuary, that
I may dwell among them."*
EXODUS 25:8

As a result of Adam and Eve's fall, God was no longer able to dwell with man as He had done before. Because of Adam, *"For as by one man's disobedience many were made sinners,"* Romans 5:19a, all of mankind became sinners. The sin that occurred in the Garden of Eden had brought a curse upon mankind, causing him to be separated from a holy and righteous God who does not allow sin into His presence. Even though man had become a sinner, God's desire was still to be with him. For this to be possible, there would have to be some way for God to remove his sin. God decided to do this through the shedding of blood. As a result of man's sinful nature, a living animal would have to be sacrificed in order to make atonement for his sin, *"and without shedding of blood there is no remission"* Hebrews 9:22b.

God, being merciful and gracious, decided to extend mankind an invitation to experience His presence once again. How did He do this? By letting them build a tabernacle where they could come and present sacrifices that would blot out their sins, hence creating a way for God to dwell in their midst. God told Moses in Exodus 25:8, *"And let them make Me a sanctuary, that I may dwell among them."* God had chosen the nation of Israel to be His people (Deuteronomy 7:6) and He wanted them to build Him a sanctuary, which would be called the Tabernacle of Meeting (Exodus 27:21). The word "tabernacle" in Hebrew means dwelling place. Wow! Once again, God was going to be able to dwell with His children.

As a result of God's invitation Israel showed its willingness by immediately accepting the task. Their actions spoke louder than words, for they began taking up an offering from those who had a willing heart (Exodus 35:21). The people were so faithful in bringing supplies for the tabernacle, that Moses had to restrain them from bringing anymore (Exodus 36:5–7). They had brought more than what was needed. Remember, the Israelites were only giving back to God what He had given them through the Egyptians (Exodus 11:2, 12:36). When Israel was departing from Egypt, they followed God's command in asking them for their valuables. The Egyptians being afraid of God's wrath and wanting to get rid of the Israelites gave them whatever they asked for. It was with these valuables that

Israel would eventually construct the tabernacle. Always remember, God will never give us a task without supplying us with the means and a way to do it. Not only had God provided Israel with the materials to construct the tabernacle, but He also provided them with the people who were skilled in artistry and craftsmanship. With the material, workers, and Israel's understanding of God's desire to be with them, they began the great work of building the Tabernacle of Meeting.

As they began building the Tabernacle of Meeting, they were careful in constructing it according to the specifications they were given by God. Moses and all of Israel had realized the importance of following God's directions from Egypt. They knew that in order to experience His personal presence, they were going to have to do as God had directed. After the children of Israel finished the work of the tabernacle, God instructed Moses to set up the tabernacle on the first day of the month (Exodus 40:2). He shared with Moses concerning the arrangement of the tabernacle and its furnishings. God had an orderly plan for His tabernacle and He knew where each socket, board, bar, pillar, screen, ring, and the pieces of furniture were going to be placed. *"For God is not the author of confusion"* 1 Corinthians 14:33a. And He wants the same for us! He desires order in our lives, so that He can come and dwell with us. We find that order when our lives line up with His holy word.

Upon Moses' finished work of the tabernacle as specified by God, it was covered with a cloud and the tabernacle was filled with the glory of the Lord (Exodus 40:34). The glory of God was so powerful that even Moses was not able to enter it. What an experience this must have been for Moses and Israel. Since Adam and Eve, there had been no person that had experienced God's personal presence in this way. God was now able, because of the tabernacle, to come and be with His people, as long as Israel kept it in order.

God shared with Moses that He would meet with him above the mercy seat. *"And there I will meet with you, and I will speak with you from above the mercy seat, from between the two cherubim which are on the ark of the Testimony,"* Exodus 25:22. The mercy seat was the Ark of the Covenant described in Exodus 25:10–22, which was placed in the Most Holy place of the Tabernacle. *"Then you shall bring the ark of the Testimony in there, behind the veil. The veil shall be a divider for you between the holy place and the Most Holy."* Exodus 26:33. Since the ark of the Testimony was the very resting place of God, it was important that Israel handle it carefully. If they were to look at or touch the ark of Testimony or go into the Most Holy place at the wrong time, they would die (1 Samuel 6:19, Numbers 4:20, 2 Samuel 6:6–7, Leviticus 16:2).

When they did approach the ark of the Testimony, it was to sprinkle it with blood once a year on the Day of Atonement. This was when the priest would make atonement for all of Israel's sins on the *"seventh month and the tenth day"* Leviticus 17:29. The high priest had the responsibility of going before God's presence on behalf of all Israel and sprinkling goat's blood on the ark of Testimony (Leviticus 16:15–16). This very act is what enabled Israel the opportunity of experiencing God's presence. And the scriptures do show that God did meet with Moses, *"Now when Moses went into the tabernacle of meeting to speak with Him, he heard the voice of One speaking to him from above the mercy seat that was on the ark of the Testimony, from between the two cherubim; thus He spoke to him."* Leviticus 7:89. Because of Moses' and Israel's obedience, God was able to come and meet with them.

God also met with Israel at the door of the

tabernacle. *"This shall be a continual burnt offering throughout your generations at the door of the tabernacle of meeting before the LORD, where I will meet you to speak with you. And there I will meet with the children of Israel . . . So I will consecrate the tabernacle of meeting and the altar. I will also consecrate both Aaron and his sons to minister to Me as priests. I will dwell among the children of Israel and will be their God."* Exodus 29:42–45. This burnt offering was a very important offering for Israel to observe. They were to take a bull in the morning and another in the evening and offer them to God on the altar to receive forgiveness for their sins. This was done daily to provide consecration for Aaron and his sons (Exodus 29:35–41). This very important offering provided much needed forgiveness for the sins of the priests, whom were to serve in the Tabernacle of Meeting before God. It was not only important for Israel to come to God once a year on the Day of Atonement to seek forgiveness of sins, but it also was necessary that blood be shed daily for the consecration of Israel. This is the way it should be for us who are children of God. God has forgiven our sins, but we still sin and come short each and every day (Romans 3:23). As a result of this, it is important that we confess our sins daily, so that we can continue to have fellowship with God. Just as God desired to meet with Israel in the Tabernacle, He wants to do the same with you and me. But we have to be sure to keep our sins confessed daily (1 John 1:9).

Just as God was present above the mercy seat and at the Tabernacle door, He was also over the Tabernacle of Meeting. *"For the cloud of the LORD was above the tabernacle by day, and fire was over it by night, in the sight of all the house of Israel, throughout all their journeys."* Exodus 40:38. When Israel would journey, God would lead them in the direction they were to go, giving them the privilege of having His presence go with them. In Numbers chapter 9 verses 15–23, we read the account of when Israel was to remain encamped or to move forward at God's command. When God moved during the day in the cloud or the fire by night, they followed. As well, when God did not move, they stayed. Whether He was in the cloud by day or the fire by night, Israel could look up and be assured of His presence in their camp. And as long as they remained obedient to His leadership, He was able to dwell in their midst.

It did not matter how far they had to travel, how high the mountain, or how low the valley they had to cross, God was there with them every step of the way. And it is the same way with us today. Sometimes we ask the question, "Where did God go?" What we need to understand is that God never leaves us, we leave Him. There have been many times in my life I have asked Him this question, and God has always gently responded to me in my heart saying, "I have been right here the whole time, waiting for you to come back." Is this something God may be telling you today? Have you moved? If so, God wants to dwell with you, but you have to go back to where you left Him. Then you must allow Him the chance to lead you in your journey here on earth (Proverbs 3:5–6).

Not only did God travel with Israel, but He also was present with them during the battles that they fought. God shared with Joshua, *"Have I not commanded you? Be strong and of good courage; do not be afraid, nor be dismayed, for the LORD your God is with you wherever you go."* Joshua 1:9. Israel was about to enter the Promise Land, and receive God's inheritance for their lives. It was important for them to realize that God was not only with them in the good times, but He also was with them when life presented challenges. In

Joshua chapter 6, we have the story of how the wall of Jericho fell. It is a great miracle of how God gave Israel the victory due to their obedience. The key to their victory is found in Joshua 6:9, *"The armed men went before the priests who blew the trumpets, and the rear guard came after the ark, while the priests continued blowing the trumpets."* If you will notice the ark of the Testimony was between the two groups of armed people, meaning that it was in the very center of the procession. Believer, when we make God the very center of our lives, we are going to see walls fall all around us. What wall or battle is keeping you from moving forward today? I want to assure you whatever it may be, God wants to help you get through it, and He will be with you as you move forward (Hebrews 13:5).

Some years later, Solomon built a permanent temple to house the furniture and the ark of the Testimony. Upon its completion and after the priest came out of the Holy Place, the temple was filled with the glory of the Lord and all of Israel saw the cloud of God's presence (1 Kings 8:4–13). God had filled the new temple with His glory just as he had the Tabernacle of Meeting. In Solomon's prayer of dedication he asked, *"But will God indeed dwell on the earth? Behold, heaven and the heaven of heavens cannot contain You. How much less this temple which I have built!"* 1 Kings 8:27. What a prayer! And the answer was yes! God would and He did, and He still does today.

As time passed, Solomon got away from the Lord and eventually Israel followed along by abandoning God's temple, ultimately rejecting His presence with them. As a result of their disobedience, God sent them into Babylonian captivity for seventy years and the temple was destroyed (2 Chronicles 36:18–21). After their captivity in Babylon, God brought them back to the Promise Land where they constructed another temple (Haggai 2). This was the same temple that was in Jerusalem during the time of Jesus. While they did experience restoration, Israel was still struggling in their sins. They were still having to give sacrifices and offerings in order to experience God's presence. And because they neglected the temple, God was having a very difficult time dwelling with them, but it wasn't going to stay that way for long.

CHAPTER 3

The Word Became Flesh

"And the Word became flesh
and dwelt among us, and we beheld
His glory, the glory as of the only begotten
of the Father, full of grace and truth."
JOHN 1:14

A s a result of Israel's disobedience, God decided to make a new covenant that would replace the old one. *"For if that first covenant had been faultless, then no place would have been sought for a second. Because finding fault with them, He says: "Behold, the days are coming, says the LORD, when I will make a new covenant with the house of Israel and with the house of Judah- not according to the covenant that I made with their fathers in the day when I took them by the hand to lead them out of the land of Egypt; because they did not continue in My covenant, and I disregarded them, says the LORD."* Hebrews 8:7–9. Because Israel "did not continue" in God's covenant they were not experiencing His presence as they did before, but that still did not keep God from wanting to be with them. God's desire to be with His people was just as strong as it had ever been.

And because His desire was still the same, He decided to send His Son Jesus Christ to earth to dwell with mankind. *"And the Word (Jesus) became flesh and dwelt among us,"* John 1:14a. His love for His creation had not changed, it had only become more personal (John 3:16). He truly was and is the Son of God, but He also was the Son of Man, (Matthew 18:11) because He was born of a virgin in Bethlehem (Matthew

1:23, Micah 5:2, Luke 2:11). It is important to understand that Jesus was completely God, but also completely man. Jesus had emotions, felt pain, was hungry, needed rest, and did die on the cross. *"For we do not have a High Priest who cannot sympathize with our weaknesses, but was in all points tempted as we are, yet without sin."* Hebrews 4:15. What an encouragement this should be to you and me. I want to encourage you by reminding you that Christ knows exactly what you are going through or what you have been through. Whether it is temptation, trials, troubles, or pain, Jesus knows exactly how you feel, and He is available to help you (Matthew 11:28–30).

In order for Jesus to come and dwell with man, it meant that He would have to leave a beautiful and perfect place called heaven. *"For you know the grace of our Lord Jesus Christ, that though He was rich, yet for your sakes He became poor, that you through His poverty might become rich."* 2 Corinthians 8:9. Just imagine, Jesus gave up all the glories of heaven to come and dwell with sinners in a sinful world. What love the Savior had shown His creation by becoming one of them and choosing to walk along side them. It meant sacrifice and devotion, and that is exactly what Jesus gave. *"just as the Son of Man did not come to be served, but to serve, and to give His life a ransom for many."* Matthew 20:28. It was customary in Bible times for the master to be served not to serve, but Jesus did the opposite. It is awesome to know that we serve a Savior, who has first served us.

What must it have been like for the disciples and Israel to experience Jesus' personal presence in their daily lives? Immanuel, which is translated "God with us" (Matthew 1:23), had become a living reality to them. They talked, handled, ate, fellowshipped, grieved, celebrated, and experienced many things with Him. God was no longer a distant Father, but now He was in their very midst. One would have thought that Jesus would have hung around the religious crowd, but Jesus ate with Publicans, tax collectors, and sinners. Jesus was questioned about this once from the religious people and responded, *"Those who are well have no need of a physician, but those who are sick."* Matthew 9:12. Jesus had come to save Israel and the world from its sins. Jesus also spent time with children, women, and even Samaritans, which were all religious wrongs for a Jew to practice. Thanks be to God that Jesus was for the underdog because we were all born sinners. Not only did He come just for the people of that time, but He came also for you and me.

Some received Him joyfully while others rejected Him (Isaiah 53:3). The very followers of God, whom we would think would have believed Him, questioned who He was. Remember, these were the very people who claimed to be God's chosen people. They knew the scriptures, the law, and were in the temple daily giving alms and prayers. Yet, they never recognized Jesus as the Messiah but ended up having Him crucified. The question that we have to ask ourselves is, "Are we living our lives in such a way that Christ feels rejected, or are we living it in a way that makes Him feel received?" If we're not careful, we can easily get caught up in the race of this life and unknowingly leave Jesus, who wants to be with us out of our lives.

God did not only send His son to dwell with man, but He sent Him to be the supreme sacrifice for his sins. God knew that humanity was dying in its sin, and the only way for it to have a chance was through a perfect sacrifice. In the Old Testament, Israel would have to give sacrifices everyday for their sins. But Jesus came to give one sacrifice (His life) that would last for eternity. *"who does not need daily, as those high priests, to offer up sacrifices, first for His own sins and then for the people's, for this He did once for all when He offered up Himself."* Hebrews 7:27. God knew the only way He could dwell with His creation like He wanted was through giving His Son. *"But God demonstrates His own love toward us, in that while we were still sinners, Christ died for us."* Romans 5:8. If this is not love, then I don't know what it would be. *"For He made Him who knew no sin to be sin for us, that we might become the righteousness of God in Him."* 2 Corinthians 5:9. It must have been very tough for Jesus to be separated from God while He was on the cross. At that point in time, He bore every sin that has ever been committed. And without a doubt we can rest assured that while He was there, we were on His mind.

After Jesus' excruciating death, His followers became more depressed and discouraged about the events that had taken place. Jesus had told them that after three days He would rise (Luke 24:7). Although they had heard Him speak of this, they never really grasped what He meant. All they knew was, Jesus "God in the flesh" who had just been with them and celebrated Passover, was now gone, and they could not understand why. It was not until after He arose from the grave, defeating all of death and hell (1Corinthians 15), that His disciples really understood what exactly had happened. Man's sin debt had been paid in full, and God's will had been done. Praise be to God; Jesus paid it all.

Jesus appeared many different times to His followers after His resurrection. On one occasion He appeared to His disciples, and showed them His nail scarred hands, feet, and the scar on His side (John 20:27). Some say, the only man made thing in heaven will be the scars on Jesus, and we are all responsible. He also ate food in front of His disciples (Luke 24:42), proving that

He had truly risen with a glorified body. And just as Jesus rose from the dead, so will we at His appearing (1 Corinthians 15:51–54). Oh what a day that will be, when we shall become as He is (1 John 3).

God did not only send His son to dwell with mankind and to die for their sins, but God also received His Son back, so that He could better dwell with His creation. Just before Christ's death, He shared with His disciples that He would be going away and that they could not come. *"A little while, and you will not see Me; and again a little while, and you will see Me, because I go to the Father."* John 16:16. This was puzzling to the disciples, since they were thinking that Christ was going to establish His kingdom on the earth at that time. They wondered where He was going, and when He would set up His kingdom. Jesus knew that their hearts were troubled after telling them these things, so He shared that it would be to their advantage that He do so. *"But because I have said these things to you, sorrow has filled your heart. Nevertheless I tell you the truth. It is to your advantage that I go away; for if I do not go away, the Helper will not come to you; but if I depart, I will send Him to you."* John 16:6–7. He was speaking of the Holy Spirit, since He knew that His physical body could only be at one place at one time. Yes, Jesus was God, but remember He was also man, and that placed him under human limitations (John 11:14). Yes, He had the power to speak and heal over distances, but He was not there in physical person (Matthew 8:1–13). But the idea was that if He ascended to the Father, then He could send the Holy Spirit who would be with them at all times.

Jesus had completed His task and upon leaving earth to go to the Father, He gave His disciples instructions, *"He commanded them not to depart from Jerusalem, but to wait for the*

Promise of the Father, 'which,' He said, 'you have heard from Me; for John truly baptized with water, but you shall be baptized with the Holy Spirit not many days from now.'" Acts 1:4–5. As His disciples and some of His followers watched Him ascend, they probably were pondering as to when they would see Him again and when they would receive the Holy Spirit. We know according to the scriptures, they did return to Jerusalem and were in the upper room where they prayed and waited for the promise. Once again God's creation was not experiencing His full presence, but it was not going to stay that way for long.

CHAPTER 4

The Spirit of Truth

"the Spirit of truth,
whom the world cannot receive,
because it neither sees Him nor knows Him;
but you know Him, for He
dwells with you and will be in you."
JOHN 14:17

The Day of Pentecost was quickly approaching and the disciples had made special preparations to get together (Acts 2:1). They had been looking and praying for the Promise of the Holy Spirit with the understanding that the time was very near (Acts 1:5). Before Jesus' death and resurrection He had told them that the Holy Spirit would come and dwell in them, *"the Spirit of truth, whom the world cannot receive, because it neither sees Him nor knows Him; but you know Him, for He dwells with you and will be in you."* John 14:17.

Although the disciples had the Holy Spirit's presence with them, they had not yet experienced Him within. This could only happen by the sending and filling of the Holy Spirit. *"And suddenly there came a sound from heaven, as of a rushing mighty wind, and it filled the whole house where they were sitting. Then there appeared to them divided tongues, as of fire, and one sat upon each of them. And they were all filled with the Holy Spirit . . . "*Acts 2:2–4. Finally the moment had arrived that God and the disciples had been looking forward to with such joy. God was now fully dwelling within His children. This was why He created mankind in the beginning, and now

He could be with all of His people, all of the time, anywhere.

As a result of this, the disciples' lives had been radically changed, never to be the same again. They now had the same Spirit in them that had raised Jesus from the dead. *"But if the Spirit of Him who raised Jesus from the dead dwells in you, He who raised Christ from the dead will also give life to your mortal bodies through His Spirit who dwells in you."* Romans 8:11. Amen! And this goes for us as well; we also have the same Spirit within us. Isn't encouraging to know we have this power within us? *"You are of God, little children, and have overcome them, because He who is in you is greater than he who is in the world."* I John 4:4.

The exciting promise of the Holy Spirit had finally come, but this was just the beginning. What they would experience in the days and years to come would only help them grow closer in their relationship with God. Their bodies were now the "temple of the Holy Spirit." *"Or do you not know that your body is the temple of the Holy Spirit who is in you, whom you have from God, and you are not your own?"* 1 Corinthians 6:19. It was no longer necessary for God's people to go to the temple since they had become the temple. How awesome it must have been for God's people to experience His presence in a new and powerful way. And what is even more wonderful is that you and I experience the same Holy Spirit each and every day. The question that we have to ask ourselves is, "Are we letting him reign or reside in our lives?" Just because He resides within us, does not mean that He reigns. If you're not letting Him reign in your life today, I want to challenge you to let Him. By doing so, you will begin to see an immediate difference, and your life will never be the same.

Not only were they the "temple of the

Holy Spirit," but they were also His vessels. *"But we have this treasure in earthen vessels, that the excellence of the power may be of God and not of us."* 2 Corinthians 4:7. The disciples were now carrying the Holy Spirit to people that needed Jesus. In order for the disciples to know where they needed to go, the Holy Spirit would direct them. *"However, when He, the Spirit of truth, has come, He will guide you into all truth;"* John 16:13a. Just as the Israelites followed the cloud by day and the pillar of fire by night, now the disciples were following the leadership of the Holy Spirit. The idea is two-fold, we carry the Holy Spirit everywhere we go and also we are to be led by the Holy Spirit. I would like to ask you two questions. Are you being led of the Holy Spirit in everything you do? And are you carrying the Holy Spirit the way you should? Remember that we are the only Jesus this lost world will ever see.

Not only did the disciples as individuals experience the Holy Spirit's presence, but they also experienced Him as a group of unified believers called the church. Just as God was dwelling with them individually, He was also dwelling with them as a whole. *"Do you not know that you are the temple of God and that the Spirit of God dwells in you?"* 1 Corinthians 3:16). You is "υμιν" [1.] in the Greek and is in the plural form, meaning that Paul was speaking to the church as a whole.

The Holy Spirit had brought unity to the early church and He was building them into a great dwelling place. *"but fellow citizens with the saints and members of the household of God, having been built on the foundation of the apostles and prophets, Jesus Christ Himself being the chief cornerstone, in whom the whole building, being joined together, grows into a holy temple in the Lord, in whom you also are being built together for a dwelling place of God in the Spirit."* Ephesians 2:19–22. And God is still building His church one brick (Christian) at a time today. I want to encourage you with this thought as a believer. You are a vital part of God's house, and without you there would be an empty place in God's house (Hebrews 10:25). You are needed just as every brick that is used in building a house. God so much wants us to be a part of His church, *"For where two or three are gathered together in my name, I am there in the midst of them."* Matthew 18:20.

Not only did the disciples have the privilege of being filled with the Holy Spirit, which resulted in experiencing His personal presence as individuals and as a church. They also were experiencing His presence twenty four hours a day, seven days a week. *"For He Himself has said, "I will never leave you nor forsake you."* Hebrews 13:5b. No matter what they were facing or going through, the disciples had the comfort of knowing that Jesus was with them. God could now be with His people anytime and anywhere. Whether in jails, mission trips, persecutions, death, famines, or trials before kings, they had the comfort of His presence. And it is the same way with you and me today.

Maybe you're dealing with something difficult today. I want to assure you that the Holy Spirit is with you, and He is willing to help you. Sometimes when we are going through difficult times, we feel that He isn't with us because we can't see Him. In the Old Testament, Moses was on Mt. Sinai with God. It was cloudy and dark and he could not see Him. *"Now the LORD descended in the cloud and stood with him there, and proclaimed the name of the LORD."* Exodus 34:5. But just because he could not see God, did not mean that the He was not there. Keep in mind that the Lord "descended" down from heaven to be with

Moses and Israel. Sometimes life is going to get dark and cloudy and we are going to have to go through some storms. But always remember, just because we can't see Him, doesn't mean that He isn't with us. And may we remember what Jesus told His disciples, *"and lo, I am with you always, even to the end of the age." Amen."* Matthew 28:20. Believer, if we will be still and listen, we can hear Him still speaking these words to our hearts today.

Not only did the disciples have the comfort of His presence twenty-four hours a day and seven days a week, but they also had His instruction and guidance in remembering what they were to be about. *"But the Helper, the Holy Spirit, whom the Father will send in My name, He will teach you all things, and bring to your remembrance all things that I said to you."* John 14:26. After the Holy Spirit came, they could also look to Him for wisdom in making decisions.

How hard would it have been for the disciples to remember all of the important truths that Jesus had taught them. Since they no longer had Jesus around to help them to know what to do, the Holy Spirit had become their teacher.

This is how the gospel writers were able to write the four gospels down. It was very important that they wrote it down correctly, and that is just what they did. We have the very word of God today because of the Holy Spirit's inspiration on their lives. Remember, the same Holy Spirit that the disciples had within them is the same that you and I have today. He speaks to our hearts through His word and His messengers. We have His 100% undivided attention when it comes to knowing what we need to do. He will see us through until the work is completed.

And just as the disciples were faced with tough decisions, we can expect to have some ourselves. It is during these times that we must be led by the abiding Holy Spirit. You and I can't go wrong if we listen to what He is telling us to do each and every day. I have always made it a priority to listen and to do what the Holy Spirit says to me. Sometimes I have plans to get such and such done on a particular day, but He leads me in a whole different direction. I look back at that day and see that if I would have done want I wanted to do, I would have missed out on a great blessing. *"A man's heart plans his way, But the LORD directs his steps."* Proverbs 16:9. How true this is in the lives of God's children. We have to plan, but God will ultimately lead us where He wants us to go. Are you willing to let Him lead you today? If so, you will go places and do things for the Lord you have never imagined possible.

CHAPTER 5

The One who Sits on the Throne

*"Therefore they are before the throne of God,
and serve Him day and night in His temple.
And He who sits on the throne
will dwell among them."*
REVELATION 7:15

The heavenly scene takes place in the future during the Great Tribulation while the church has been removed from the earth. At this point we will be with the Lord who is seated on the throne with those who have come out of the Great Tribulation (Revelation 7:14). Most Christians agree and believe that the church will not go through the Tribulation spoken of in the book of Revelation. Tim Lahaye, co-author of the *Left Behind* series shares concerning this, "There are sixteen references to the Church in Revelation 1–3, whereas chapters 6–18, which cover the Tribulation, do not mention the Church once. The natural conclusion drawn from this is that the Church was so prominent during its two thousand-year history (as predicted in chapters 2–3) is not mentioned in chapters 4–18 because those chapters describe the Tribulation, which the church does not endure." [2.]

The Great Tribulation is the seven year period when God will pour out His judgment on the earth. It will take place after Jesus comes and takes His church home. Jesus shared with His disciples that He would one day come back for them and His church (John 14:3). This future event has been called the rapture. The word "rapture" comes from the Latin and it means to be caught up. So when Jesus comes back for His church we will be caught up and meet Him in the sky.

There are two familiar passages in the Bible that speak of the rapture of the church, 1 Corinthians 15:51–52 and 1 Thessalonians 4:16–17. We also know Jesus made several statements concerning His return for His church. And in these, He warned them to be ready for His coming at anytime. While some say Jesus is not coming back for His church. We must as Paul shared in Titus 2:13, *"keep looking for the blessed hope and glorious appearing of our great God and Savior Jesus Christ,"* And just as they were looking for the rapture in Paul's time, we are to be looking for it today. Some have tried to pin a date on the rapture, but even the Bible shares that no one but the Father knows when the rapture will happen (Matthew 24:36). With this we must take careful heed to what Jesus said, *"Therefore you also be ready, for the Son of Man is coming at an hour you do not expect."* Matthew 24:44. Are you ready if He were to come today? If not, why don't you pray and receive Him before it's too late.

It is after the rapture and during the Great Tribulation that God will also dwell with us in heaven. *"Therefore they are before the throne of God, and serve Him day and night in His temple. And He who sits on the throne will dwell among them."* Revelation 7:15. Amazing, even in heaven God will still be dwelling with His creation. One would think that it should be said that we will dwell with Him. But God never changes; He is the same always (Hebrews 13:8). He has dwelt, is dwelling, and will dwell with His creation.

What is it going to be like in heaven during this time? No one really knows other than what the Bible shares. One thing is for sure, it is going to be the best worship service we have ever been in. We will be there worshipping with

those who have come "out of the great tribulation" (Revelation 7:14). And just as these will be
before His throne, so shall we. What a wonderful day it is going to be when we're all gathered
together sitting at the feet of Jesus.

We see a picture of this in Revelation 4:10,
*"the twenty-four elders fall down before Him who
sits on the throne and worship Him who lives forever and ever, and cast their crowns before the
throne."* One day we will have the opportunity to
cast our crowns at the feet of Jesus. The believer
is going to be given rewards in heaven, some
of which will be crowns. These various crowns
are spoken of throughout the Bible and will be
rewarded to those who have fulfilled the require-
ments to attain them. Along with them, we are
to be laying up treasures in heaven (Matthew
6:20). When we do receive all that He has for us
in heaven, we will in return, humbly bow down
and place it at His nail scarred feet, only to be

reminded of the price that He paid for us to be there with Him. For He is worthy of all praise, honor and glory. I want to ask you a question. Are you laying up treasures in heaven? If so, I want to encourage you to continue the good work. But if not, I want to encourage you to start today. Your retirement on earth may or may not be much, but you can rest assured that if you invest your life in serving God, your retirement will be out of this world.

We will be there day and night serving Him in His temple (Revelation. 7:15). There are twelve references in the book of Revelation concerning the temple in heaven including this one. The temple that is spoken of in Revelation has some of the same type of furnishings that were used in the Tabernacle of Meeting in Exodus. The writer of Hebrews speaks more about this, *"who serve the copy and shadow of the heavenly things, as Moses was divinely instructed when he was about to make the tabernacle. For He said, "See that you make all things according to the pattern shown you on the mountain."* Hebrews 8:5. It may be that the Tabernacle of Meeting that Moses built was similar to the one in heaven. God may have wanted it this way so that He could come and dwell with the Israelites. We can't be completely sure of this, but it would have to be heavenly for God to come and dwell in it.

The same is true with the church today. If we are going to experience His presence in a stronger way, we are going to have to offer Him true worship like He is receiving day and night in heaven. The reason that churches and believers aren't experiencing His full presence today like they should is because they are not truly welcoming and worshipping Him. Why would God want to come to a place where He does not feel welcome? We must remember, God's desire to meet with us when we come together for church is more powerful than we would ever know (Matthew 18:20). All that God has ever wanted is to be with His children and for His children to want to be with Him. This takes place when His people seek Him through worship. *"God is Spirit, and those who worship Him must worship in spirit and truth."* John 4:24.

After the seven years of Tribulation, Jesus will ride back to earth on a white horse with the armies of heaven (us) to wipe out the Antichrist and the False Prophet along with all of his followers. Then He will then set up His kingdom on earth and reign for a thousand years while Satan is bound (Revelation 19–20). This is called the Second Coming and several passages in the Bible speak concerning this event. Some examples are Matthew chapter 24, Mark chapter 13, Luke chapter 21, and the Major and Minor Prophet books of the Old Testament.

When Jesus ascended to heaven in Acts

1:10–12, the angels shared, *"'Men of Galilee, why do you stand gazing up into heaven? This same Jesus, who was taken up from you into heaven, will so come in like manner as you saw Him go into heaven.' Then they returned to Jerusalem from the mount called Olivet, which is near Jerusalem,"* This is in reference to His Second Coming. The Old Testament passages that correlates with this is Zechariah 14:4, *"And in that day His feet will stand on the Mount of Olives, which faces Jerusalem on the east. And the mount of Olives shall be split in two, From east to west,"* The rest of this chapter deals with the outcome of His Second Coming.

His first coming was as a babe in Bethlehem and led to Him giving His life on the cross to set up His spiritual kingdom. But His second coming will not be the same. This time it will not be as a babe, but as the conquering "King of Kings and Lord of Lords" to set up His earthly kingdom.

"Behold, He is coming with clouds, and every eye will see Him, even they who pierced Him. And all the tribes of the earth will mourn because of Him. Even so, Amen." Revelation 1:7.

CHAPTER 6

The Millennium Reign

"And He said to me, "Son of man, this is the place of My throne and the place of the soles of My feet, where I will dwell in the midst of the children of Israel forever."

EZEKIEL 43:7A

After Jesus comes back and sets up His kingdom, we will reign with Him here on earth for a thousand years (Revelation 20:6). This time period is referred to as the Millennium Reign. Most scholars agree that it will occur after Christ's Second Coming and will be a literal thousand years. They also agree that the prophet Ezekiel wrote concerning this future event in Ezekiel chapters 40–48. Tim Lahaye shares, "Then in chapters 40–48 we encounter a description of the millennial kingdom, particularly the temple and conditions for worship during that thousand-year period." [3.] There is a lot that we don't understand about these nine chapters, but what we do understand really encourages us. We do know that this is going to be a very peaceful and happy time. The earth will experience true peace for the first time since the fall of man in the Garden of Eden.

But what is most amazing is that God will once again be dwelling in our midst. *"And He said to me, 'Son of man, this is the place of My throne and the place of the soles of My feet, where I will dwell in the midst of the children of Israel forever.'"* Ezekiel 43:7a. One would think again that we would be the ones dwelling with Him, but this will not be the case. Just as Jesus is dwelling and will dwell with us during the Tribulation, He is also going to do the same during the Millennium.

Jesus spoke of His kingdom many times in the four gospels, and gave a command for His believers to seek that kingdom (Matthew 6:33). When He was standing before Pilate for the accusation of claiming to be the "King of the Jews," He shared that His kingdom was not of this world (John 18:36a). His kingdom was in heaven at that time, but one day He will come and set it up here on earth. The model prayer given to the disciples by Jesus instructed them to pray, *"Our Father in heaven, Hallowed be Your name. Your kingdom come."* Matthew 6:9–10. This prayer has been prayed many times since Jesus gave it. Our desire as children of God should be to see His kingdom come. For when this happens, evil will be removed and their will be a restoration of righteousness. When it does come to pass we will have the experience of being a part of it.

Right now Jesus is at the right hand of God who is seated on the throne. The Bible shares *"neither by heaven, for it is God's throne; "nor by the earth, for it is His footstool;"* Matthew 5:34b-35a. Ezekiel 43:7 states that the earth will be God's throne and His footstool. Imagine heaven on earth and that is what it is going to be like in His kingdom. Right now the world is in the worse condition that it has ever been, and it is not going to get any better. Regardless of what the news and media says, immorality is on the rise and mankind is becoming more wicked by the day. The world is Satan's domain for now, and he is doing everything he can to turn it completely against God. It may seem that he is winning right now, but we can be assured by God's word that his days are numbered.

We see this in Revelation 20:1–2, where an angel is going to take Satan and cast him down into the pit and seal him in for a thousand year period. Finally that serpent of old will be off of the earth for a thousand years. It is going to be wonderful not to have to deal with him or his demons. There will be no more murder, war, racism, drugs, sexual immorality, sickness, disease, and the list could go on and on. It will literally be heaven on earth. And after the thousand years, Satan will be loosed for a season to make one last shot at God and His people, only to be cast into the lake of fire for eternity (Revelation 20:10). This is a day that I would say all of God's children can't wait to see happen, and what a good riddance it will be.

Not only will we have the experience of being in His kingdom, but we will also have the honor of having Him as King. The world we live in today has kings that rule over provinces or kingdoms. They live in luxury and have the privilege to do as they please. Some rule with goodness while others are wicked, but one day this world is going to have the true King ruling over it, whose name is Jesus (Psalm 2:9). As His children we are going to be able to enjoy all of the benefits and luxuries that He has to offer (1 John 3:1). Have you ever wondered what it would be like to be the child of a king, to experience all the glory and splendor that comes with being a part of royalty, to live in a castle and know that your financial future is taken care of, as well as your children's children, to have servants to wait on you hand and foot, to never have to work, to not have to wash clothes or dishes or pick up around the house? The list could go on and on. Wouldn't that be wonderful?

With that thought, I want to share a story with you—one I have never forgotten that my grandparents once told me. My grandfather served in the Korean Conflict with men from all over the United States. Many years after his discharge, he went to a reunion to see some of his old navy buddies, only to discover that one of them had become a king. What had happened was, unknowingly, this guy was in the lineage of a king's family from an African nation. After coming out of the service, he began to delve into his family tree, and to His amazement he found out that he was a royal descendant. This led him to go to that nation and to eventually be crowned as their king. He and his wife came to the reunion all dressed up in their royal attire and showed proof of his kingship. This is something that just doesn't happen every day. To be a child of an earthly king is a very unique privilege since you have to be born into it. The throne can only be passed down through blood. And that is exactly what happened to you and me. We became children of the King as a result of Jesus' shed blood. It was only through His precious blood that our sins were washed away and we were born again. Although it would be very unique and advantageous to have an earthly king as a father, it doesn't hold any comparison to being a child of King Jesus.

Not only will we have the privilege of having him as King, but we will also reign with Him during the Millennium. The Bible states in Revelation 20:6, that His people will reign with Him. And it also says, *"and has made us kings and priests to His God and Father, to Him be glory and dominion forever and ever. Amen."* Revelation 1:6. Just think, one day we will be kings. Tim Lahaye shares, "We may not look like kings today, but there is a day coming when, because we are the children of God by faith, we will rule and reign with Him-" [4.]

The average person today does not really have a say as to what is being done in the world. Our local and world governments determine this. We are just one voice among many, and unless we hold a prominent position, we will probably never be heard. But I want to assure you, it will not always be like this. A day is coming when as kings we will have a say that matters. Right now the world has no respect for God or us as Christians. Jesus once said, *"If the world hates you, you know that it hated Me before it hated you."* John 15:18. The world has always hated true Christians and it will never change. Our faith is being scrutinized more now than ever. Various people are trying to have Jesus and God removed from everything. They have already taken Him out of our schools and some of our court rooms. And now they are trying to have His name removed from statues, monuments, public meetings, and our money.

Although we are taking a stand, it is really hard for us to do anything since we don't make the deciding vote as an elected official can. But we can contact them and let them know where we stand. Until Jesus sets up His kingdom on the earth, the world is only going to get worse and worse, but the good news is we win in the end because of what Jesus did at Calvary and one day we will be royalty and the earth will be ours forever. *"Blessed are the meek, For they shall inherit the earth,"* Matthew 5:5.

CHAPTER 7

The Tabernacle of God

"And I heard a loud voice from heaven saying,
"Behold, the tabernacle of God is with men,
and He will dwell with them, and they shall be
His people. God Himself will be
with them and be their God."
REVELATION 21:3

A new heaven and earth will be ushered in after the Millennium period. The Great White Throne judgment will have taken place and Death and Hades will have been cast into the lake of fire (Revelation 20:14–15). John saw this new heaven and earth along with the New Jerusalem coming down out of heaven in Revelation chapter 21. The old heaven and earth will have passed away (Revelation 20:11). After this vision he received a word from heaven, *"And I heard a loud voice from heaven saying, "Behold, the tabernacle of God is with men, and He will dwell with them, and they shall be His people. God Himself will be with them and be their God."* Revelation 21:3. Wow! Once again God will be dwelling with His people, and it will be forever. Just think about it. One day we are going to experience all the glory and splendor of being on a new heaven and earth, and God is going to be in our midst.

As finite beings, we will never be able to comprehend eternity. The thought of living forever and ever can boggle the human mind. God is, has always been, and always will be. Once we as believers die, we will live forever with God, having no end. The Bible shares, *"with the Lord one day is as a thousand years, and a thousand years as one day."* 2 Peter 3:8b. God's time is definitely not the same as ours. While we use calendars and clocks to keep up with dates and time, before creation there was no time. God spoke and it all began. The first clocks and calendars were spun into existence with the sun, moon, and stars, but one day there will no more need for these. *"There shall be no night there: They need no lamp nor light of the sun, for the Lord God gives them light."* Revelation 22:5a. Just think; it will be a day without end.

Have you ever had a day that you thought would never end—one of those days where nothing went right? It seemed the hands of time were at a stand still, and when the sunset came, it was a pleasant reminder that the troublesome day was finally over. On the other hand, have you ever had the perfect day—one you wished would never end? You were with the perfect person, in the perfect place, at the perfect time. Only then the hands of time seemed to move more quickly than normal. Before you knew it the sun was setting, signaling the end of a day that you could never live again. When the sun sets on our troubled life here, we will finally be in the perfect place with the perfect person, and there will be no more time. For all of eternity our Savoir will dwell with us in the place He is creating for us, and we will never see another sunset.

From exercising, anti-aging drugs, to plastic surgery, people today are doing everything humanly possible to stay young. They are trying to stop a natural process called dying. Once we are born, we immediately start to die, and no matter how much science and technology advances, it will never offer eternal youth and vitality. The world we live in has always feared the hereafter since they don't know where it leads. For the unbeliever death is the end and an eternal hell awaits them, but to the believer death is only the beginning. As the Apostle Paul shared, *"For to me, to live is Christ, and to die is gain."* Philippians 1:21.

In heaven we will have healthy vibrant bodies and will never have to worry about growing old or getting sick. There will be no nursing homes, hospitals, dental offices, or funeral homes there. But while we are on earth, we will get older and eventually die unless Jesus returns. Growing older means that we are only getting closer to heaven. This earth is not our home; we are just passing through (Hebrews 11:13–14). At salvation we became justified, we are being sanctified now, and one day we will have glorified bodies. *"Beloved, now we are children of God; and it has not yet been revealed what we shall be, but we know that when He is revealed, we shall be like Him, for we shall see Him as He is."* 1 John 3:2.

Just think of it, there will also be no more need for banks, insurance companies, home improvement stores, police departments, IRS, the Department of Transportation, etc. In heaven we will have everything we need, without any debt. As a result there will be no poverty, famines, or homeless people. Unlike earth, there will be no earthquakes, tornadoes, hurricanes, tsunamis, volcanoes, avalanches, forest fires, or floods. We will have our very own mansion that will never need any repairs. There will be no down payments or security deposits with payments to follow. Because there will be no crime, alarm systems, locks, and prisons will be a thing of the past. There also will be no property, inheritance, or income taxes. And lastly since the streets will be made of gold, there will be no need for road repairs. I think we all can really appreciate this one.

We will not have to deal with alarm clocks, deadlines, and busy schedules. This is because we will have all of eternity to do the things that we neglected to do while on earth, like spending quality time with our families and friends. We are always in a rush and never take time out to enjoy life. In heaven we will have forever to spend with our love ones. There will be no need to be in a hurry and it won't matter how much time we spend, since we are all going to be together forever. What a delight it's going to be when we get to sit down and talk with the Old and New Testament saints. But most of all, we will be able to spend time with Jesus our Lord and Savior, who died for our sins, and He will spend time with us forever and ever (Revelation 20:3).

In heaven there will be no need for tissues. *"And God will wipe away every tear from their eyes; there shall be no more death, nor sorrow, nor crying. There shall be no more pain, for the former things have passed away."* Revelation 21:4. Tears symbolize sorrow or joy in the life of a human being. Even while Jesus was on earth He shed tears (John 11:35). There has been a great misconception about the shedding of tears in heaven. Some have said that there will be no tears there. The Bible shares that there will be, but God will wipe them away. We don't know everything about heaven, but what we are able to understand should encourage us. I can remember singing the song, "He's Got the Whole World in His Hands" as a child. But one day the same God that holds all of creation in His hands will wipe away every tear from our eyes. What a day it's going to be when we will have God dwelling in our midst. There will be no more sorrow ever again.

As Christians we have always wondered what it is going to be like in heaven. The only way to ever find out will be through death. And I will be the first to tell you, I'm not in a hurry to find out, but I'm really excited about going. What about you? Are you ready? If not, all you have to do is pray this prayer right now. Lord, I admit that I'm a sinner. I believe you died on the cross for my sins. Please forgive my sins and come into my heart. Amen.

THE SEVEN DWELLING PLACES OF GOD IN THE BIBLE

Creation	Old Testament	New Testament	Church Age	7 year Tribulation	1000 years on earth	New Heaven and Earth
The Garden of Eden Genesis 3.8	The Tabernacle of Meeting Exodus 25:8	The Word Became Flesh John 1:14	The Spirit of Truth John 14:17	The One Who Sits on the Throne Revelation 7:15	The Millenium Reign Ezekiel 43:7	The Tabernacle of God Revelation 21:3
1	2	3	4	5	6	7

James Stevens

CONCLUSION

There you have it, the seven dwelling places of God in the Bible. Looking back, we have seen where God was with Adam and Eve in the Garden of Eden, with Israel in the Tabernacle of Meeting, on earth dwelling with mankind, and with the disciples and us today. And in the future He will dwell with us during the seven year Tribulation, the Millennium, and on the new heaven and earth. Getting back to that cold January night in 2003, I remember when I counted the dwelling places and they added up to seven. I was absolutely amazed since seven is the perfect number. God created the heavens and the earth and rested on the seventh day, meaning completion. The number seven is used throughout the book of Revelation. It mentions seven churches (2–3), seven Spirits of God (4:5), seven seals (5:1), seven trumpets (8:6), seven thunders (10:4), and seven bowl judgments (16:1). The Tribulation period will also last seven years (Daniel 9:27). The number seven is used 433 times in the New King James Bible. Could these seven distinct dwelling places of God in the Bible be another sign of completeness? I will leave the answer up to you. What's really important for us to know is God wants to be with us. And we must be careful and not hide from His presence as Adam and Eve did.

ENDNOTES

1. Robinson, Maurice A. and Pierpont, William G., Editors, Byzantine/Majority *Text-form Greek New Testament,* (Roswell, GA: The Original Word Publishers) 1991.

2. Lahaye, Tim, *Revelation Unveiled.* Grand Rapids: Zondervan Publishing House, 1999, p. 100.

3. Ibid., p. 341.

4. Ibid., p. 31.

Contact author James Stevens
or order more copies of this book at

TATE PUBLISHING, LLC

127 East Trade Center Terrace
Mustang, Oklahoma 73064

(888) 361 - 9473

Tate Publishing, LLC

www.tatepublishing.com